Peirce James Nice

The Nine Lives of The Good Kitty
(Moving and Making New Friends)

Bumblebee Books
London

BUMBLEBEE PAPERBACK EDITION

A CIP catalogue record for this title is
available from the British Library.

ISBN: 978-1-83934-061-1

Bumblebee Books is an imprint of
Olympia Publishers.

First Published in 2021

Bumblebee Books
Tallis House
2 Tallis Street
London
EC4Y 0AB

Printed in Great Britain

www.olympiapublishers.com

Dedication

This book is dedicated to all the children who have ever had to endure the hardships and fears and utter sense of helplessness associated with a move. It is my sincere hope that this story of *The Good Kitty* will help children learn how to cope with, and ultimately embrace, the difficulties (losing friends, changing schools, and especially fear and the loss of control) children of all ages experience when a family moves. For my beautiful, dear and loving family, without whom, none of this would have been possible. Thank you for your incredible support and for teaching me how to love. I could not have had more luck. And, for everyone, anywhere, who ever feels alone in their travels, I promise you, you are not.

-

Q: What kind of question does an animal ask?
A: That is a funny question for an animal to ask

The Good Kitty was the most beautiful kitty in the entire world. His fur was like a fluffy cloud of cotton candy, with eyes like perfect blue and black marbles. He could jump higher than any other kitty, run faster than any other kitty...

…and also could break more glasses than any other kitty!

A seemingly fearless creature of amazing grace and fury.

But even the strongest and most beautiful creatures feel fear...

...when they don't have control.

Left in the dark.

P

With no way to understand what is happening.

Or why it is happening... feeling like they are just dragged around.

With no one else who understands... and with no choice.

The Good Kitty saw many places in the world, and even though he understood in his mind that this was a good thing, in his heart it hurt to always have to be the new kitty, and adjust to all the new smells and colors and different animals.

Having fear didn't make The Good Kitty a coward. In fact, having fear is what made The Good Kitty so brave, because he was able to get through it and still try to understand. This is what made him The Good Kitty.

Home is where the heart is and The Good Kitty has a heart as big as the world. The Good Kitty began realizing that anywhere could be home and that everywhere has good friends to be made.

One day a new kitty named Nina arrived.

The Good Kitty really wanted to be her friend, but she was afraid of EVERYTHING! The Good Kitty understood she just needed time, and in time they became best friends.

He told her there's no need to be afraid as long as there is love and that there is always love.

And they both learned to love their new home
and each other, very much.

But one day things were different…at least for The Good Kitty.
The Good Kitty saw boxes again!

Nina saw The Good Kitty in a way she'd never seen him before.
She saw HIM afraid!

“What's wrong? There are so many boxes to play in!” asked Nina.

“That's what is wrong! The boxes!” The Good Kitty replied.

“That's why I am scared!” exclaimed The Good Kitty.

"You!? Scared?! Of boxes!?"

“You don't understand what they mean yet... The boxes mean we will be thrown into the dark again! The boxes mean that all the time we have put into making this place our home together and all the memories we've made here are soon going to just be a thing of the past.”

"You are the one who taught me that it is okay to be afraid. And it is scary, the idea that we have to go somewhere else, but I'm not worried because we have each other. I have you and you have me.
Love is all we need to call *a place* home."

“Because home is where the heart is. Home is wherever we are together,” purred Nina.

And The Good Kitty and his new friend Nina were both afraid but both ready for new adventures, and to take on the whole world, and as long as they had love, they would always be home.

About the Author

I sincerely hope you enjoy reading this story as much as I enjoyed writing it. I myself am the son of a career soldier and longtime diplomat. We moved nine times by the time I was eighteen. I intimately know how difficult it is for a child to uproot every couple of years. I will say this with as much honesty and sincerity I can muster, I truly wish I had these types of books to help explain things to me when I was a kid. I can think of nothing more satisfying personally or professionally than knowing that if a child reads these books the distress, fear, and sense of utter helplessness felt by countless children globally could somehow be meaningfully eased, or even perhaps eliminated altogether.

These books are relevant regardless of a child's country of origin, or language. As a former child who has attended several international, and United Nations schools around the world, I can tell you with certainty that nearly every country on Earth sends its diplomats and business men and women abroad; often times accompanied by their school-age children. *Nine Lives Of The Good Kitty* was written with those families in mind.

CPSIA information can be obtained
at www.ICGtesting.com
Printed in the USA
BVRC091210210521
607789BV00010B/344